Many Leaves, One Tree

A Collection of Aphorisms

Kenneth P. Langer

Brass Bell Books

BRASS BELL
BOOKS & GAMES

Preface

When I first read the ancient book known as the Tao Te Ching I was dumbfounded. For the first time in my life, I found something that presented a view of the world that made sense to me. The Tao Te Ching is short and appears simple but it is not. It attempts to balance oppositions in thinking and in living. For many Westerners used to defining things through dichotomies, the idea that opposites are really just parts of a whole can be confounding but also liberating. It was both for me. The concise and poetic way in which the Tao Te Ching approaches its insights appealed to me and inspired me to write a collection of thoughts as well.

This work is not another translation or commentary on the Tao Te Ching. It is, instead, a collection of my thoughts inspired by that ancient book. The reader may, at times, find close parallels to the Tao Te Ching while, at other times, find sharp opposition. I make no apology. I was not trying to copy the ancient text but simply let the words flow in their own direction under the guidance of the old words. That, after all, is the way of the Tao.

Terms

The One

The source from which all things come and to which all things return. This term should not be confused with "the one" (small 'O"), or "the self."

The Way

A path of peace and contentment for the individual; a way for all people to attempt to unite with The One. It is a method for living a positive life based on a respect for the needs and desires of all people. It is a basis for living and making decisions.

The Myriad

All things: all people of all races, all living things, all inanimate objects, and all objects of this existence known or unknown.

Harmony

People living in accordance with The Way where all live with mutual respect and love for themselves, each other, and all things. Like many other subjects presented here, it is understood that such a goal may not be possible however its pursuit is, nonetheless, worthwhile.

Discord

That which goes against harmony.

Balance

Balance is a way of living in moderation. To live in balance is to reject excesses and extremes. Understanding balance means knowing that life is composed of opposites such as good and evil, love and hate, male and female, and so on. A person who lives in balance knows and accepts that these dualities exist but also understands that each of these is part of a greater wholeness and that they share a complex interdependence. Understanding these things helps one make wise decisions that can lead to a life of contentment.

For what purpose does the leaf exist? It exists to live and, in so doing, feeds the unified existence of the whole tree. The tree, in turn, exists as a leaf to the world. The leaf yearns to touch the sunlight, the wind, and the rain. By simply living and living simply it is fulfilled and by dying simply it falls to the ground and returns to the tree.

A Diagram of the Way

The following chart displays the three energies within all of us. The mind is the seat of mental energy, the body houses physical energy, and the heart houses emotional energy. Each of these can be directed in negative, neutral, or positive ways. Negative influences and actions deplete personal energy while positive influences and action increase and nourish the self. The Way of Harmony is to seek the neutral balance between positive and negative influences for each of the three channels of energy. The natural tendency of change will cause both positive and negative fluctuations in energies which is the experience of life itself. If negative times can be tolerated with patience and an openness to learning while positive times can be experienced without desire then a balanced life can be achieved.

MIND (mental energy)	BODY (physical energy)	HEART (emotional energy)	
Understand the self	Possess good health	Love of self	Positive
Understand all others	Balance of activities	Love of others	
Understand all things	Achieve full potential	Love of all things	
Know only what is needed to survive	Have only the means necessary to survive	Feel only the will to survive	Neutral
Ignorance of self	Debilitating health	Hatred of self	Negative
Ignorance of others	Excessive activity	Hatred of others	
Ignorance of all	Unfulfilled potential	Hatred of all	

The One

1.

At first the three:

That which is becoming,

That which is not becoming,

That which is not.

But all things are becoming

And all things not

Are becoming.

The three are all

The One.

2.

The One

Can neither be seen,

Nor heard,

Nor touched,

And yet

It is in all things

Seen,

Heard,

And touched.

3.

The One

Has always been

And will always be

Permanent, Unformed

While all else

Remains impermanent,

Evolving.

The unformed and the forming are the same.

4.

All are part of The One

And are innately guided by it.

Its silent call is heard only

By those who stop to listen.

5.

Being is defined from Nothingness.

Therefore to first find

The nothing of each thing

Is to find its essence.

6.

See the self as

Part of The One.

See the nation as

Part of The One.

See the myriad as

Part of The One

And all things

Will be seen clearly.

7.

Seek The One

Through the myriad

But first seek the myriad

Through the self.

No other can define the self.

8.

The One can be found

When it is not sought.

Live the day for itself,

Follow The Way,

And The One will become clear.

9.

Movement with The One

Is simple and natural.

It is often like

Remaining perfectly still.

10.

One can be advanced

Without advancing

And can be centered

Without being the center

When one realizes

The self is–

As all are–

An integral part of The One.

The Way

11.

The Way is like water.

It benefits all things

Without expectation.

It fills the low places:

Now soft,

Now strong.

It moves with the earth

And takes many forms.

It is the essence of life.

12.

The Way is a winding stream

That flows

Through a mountain woods

Between two banks

Touching every tree

That stands at its shores.

13.

The water of the stream flows gently onward:

Changing course

When change is needed,

Boring through great rock

When strength is needed.

14.

A stream likens its path.

If it cannot liken,

It will accept.

If it cannot accept,

It will alter.

If it cannot alter,

It will seek a new way

And liken its path.

15.

Strive for the harmony of

The One

By seeking

The knowledge of the self

And of all things,

The love of the self

And of all things

The potential of the self

And of all things.

16.

The Way for the body Is to seek purpose.

The Way for the mind Is to seek the truth.

The Way for the heart Is to seek unity.

The Way for the self Is to laugh.

17.

The child

Seeks to understand all it can,

Strives to love all it can,

Works to do all it can,

But grows to learn

Ignorance, hatred, and defeat.

Seek the wisdom of the child.

18.

To seek the wisdom of

The One

Is to know all things.

To seek the love of

The One

Is to love all things.

To seek the strength of

The One

Is to hold up all things.

To seek one's purpose with

The One

Is to be all things.

19.

The Way is

To Learn

To Live

To Love

To Laugh.

20.

To understand

The Way

Is to take the chance

Of not being understood,

Yet requires

That one always be

Understanding.

21.

Study the cycles of change;

Be a part of them.

Sometimes it is best

To move forward.

Sometimes it is best

To move back.

Sometimes it is best

To remain still

Knowing that

The end of one journey

Leads to another.

22.

The Way is not easy.

It requires caring,

Compassion,

And patience.

Therefore, few

Will have the strength

To walk it.

23.

The Way is to take

The mountainous path–

For only by climbing

Can one see the splendor.

24.

The walk of

The Way

Is a solitary journey

That is shared

By the myriad.

25.

True joy is found

By attaining unity

Through The One

But the journey is incredible

And contentment is found only

By striving

As best as one can.

26.

Seeking The Way in the self

Creates contentment.

Seeking The Way in all people

Creates peace.

Seeking The Way in the myriad

Creates harmony.

27.

Happiness is nothing more

Than simple contentment

In knowing

The Way

And success

Is nothing more

Than humble satisfaction

In living

The Way.

28.

Just as there will always be those

Who follow The Way–

Knowingly or unknowingly–

There will always be those

Who do not.

29.

Fear those

Who claim to see the tree

Without truly looking

At every leaf

And fear those

Who claim to see the forest

Without truly looking

At every tree.

30.

Since all came from

The One

All should seek to return

to The One.

To do so is harmony.

Harmony is The Way.

31.

Positive action

Is that which seeks unity

With The One

In accordance with

The Way.

Knowledge begins with

No thought.

Love begins with

No feeling.

Potential begins with

No action.

The Way of Knowledge

32.

Truth is defined From un-truth

Both being part of The One.

To seek the true

One must often first comprehend

The untrue.

33.

The truth may not always

Be ornate

And the ornate

May not always be truthful.

34.

The mind naturally seeks

To know all things

But to know all things

One must first know

The self-

For knowledge

Emanates

From the center.

35.

Seek answers from where

Questions reside.

To seek beyond is to seek in vain.

36.

Those who know

They do not know

Gain wisdom.

Those who claim to know

Do not

And remain ignorant.

37.

The one who thinks to know

May know the least

For no mortal can know

The immortal truth.

Therefore,

Seek to answer questions

But also seek to question

Each answer.

The Way of Love

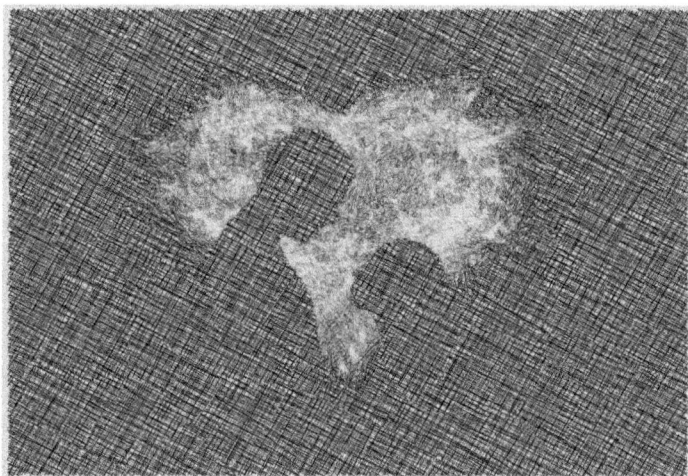

38.

To love one is to love all

To love all is to be Compassionate:

Which leads to tolerance,

Which leads to strength,

Which leads to harmony,

Which leads to The One.

39.

To seek love

Is to first love others.

To love others

Is to first love the self.

To love the self

Is to first accept what is

And what is not.

40.

The earth holds the tree

Gently

And provides what is needed.

For if it is held too tight

Or overburdened.

The tree will surely die.

41.

Grasp the water tightly

And it shall slip away.

Hold the water lightly

And it shall caress

The fingers.

42.

Love is the natural state

That binds all things.

Hush the anger,

Seek unity,

There will be love.

43.

Let the energy of the enemy

Spend itself

Until exhausted

And he falls.

Then help him to his feet.

The Way of Potential

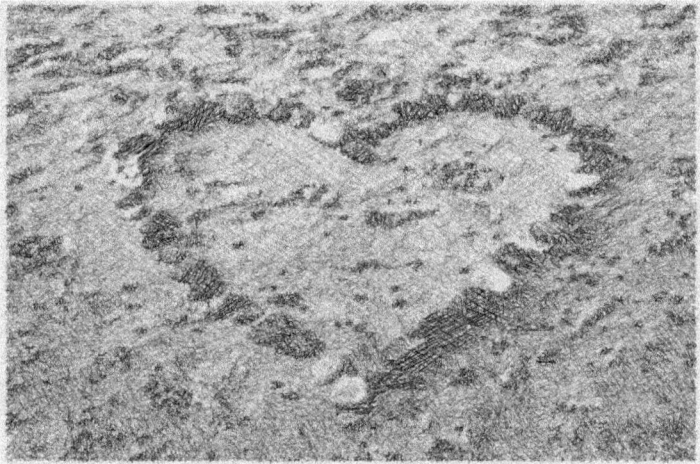

44.

When the self seeks

The One

It seeks to experience

All things:

To cry

When a cry is needed,

To sing

When a song is needed,

To laugh

When a laugh is needed,

To be silent

When silence is needed.

45.

See what can be seen

Then do not.

Touch what can be touched

Then do not.

Taste what can be tasted

Then do not.

Hear what can it be heard

Then do not.

This is living in balance.

46.

Be as the husband,

Be as the wife.

Be as the parent,

Be as the child.

Thus, the heart blossoms.

47.

Do not talk of

The Way.

No one shall listen.

Live in

The Way

And all will hear.

48.

Talk of doing

Does nothing.

Doing without talking

Creates success.

49.

The true character of the self

Is not expressed in words

But in action

And inaction.

The Self

50.

The image of The Self

Can be no greater

Than the true self

Or one will surely fall.

51.

Action for the good of the self

Against the good of all

Causes discord

And cracks the foundation

Of harmony.

52.

The energy needed

To appear to be

Detracts from

The energy needed

To be

And, thereby,

Makes one not.

53.

Success is not measured

Through the words of others.

It is found only

In the satisfaction Of the self.

54.

When the self

Is not the center

Of all things

But part of

The One

There is no need

To seek favor.

55.

The self is not defined

By its outer rim.

Seek the center

And find stability.

56.

The excess of any action

Diminishes the heart,

Diminishes the mind,

Diminishes the body,

While balance achieves harmony.

The Way is to seek balance.

57.

Calm the breath,

Quiet the mind

And gain peace

Through the beauty

Of The One.

One's center is found In the quiet depths

Of the self.

58.

A promise made and broken

Is a greater shame

Than a promise never made.

59.

The greatest treasures

Are those

That cannot be seen.

60.

A yes must remain a yes,

A no must remain a no,

Or words will have no meaning.

A principle must remain

Intact

Or life will have no meaning.

61.

If one wishes to live in Balance

According to The Way,

One must know when to do

And when not to do,

When to say yes

And when to say no.

62.

The greatest treasures

Are those buried deep within

For from without

They cannot be tarnished,

They cannot be scratched,

But shine bright as starlight.

63.
That which is deeply felt

To be true

Is certainly true.

64.

Be as the tree

That stands firm

In its roots

But dances

With the changing winds

In its leaves.

65.

That which is the source

Of the problem

Is also the source

Of the solution.

66.

A greater good

Creates a greater chance

To be vicious.

A greater wisdom

Creates a greater chance

To be ignorant.

A greater love

Creates a greater chance

To hate.

Walk steady but slow.

67.

A great mountain

Can only be conquered

By climbing simple steps

One by one.

68.

One leg may be strong

While the other weak

Though they are aware

Of the same body,

Yet one still learns to walk.

69.

Often it is best

Not to ask

Which way to go

But to put forward

The strong foot

And just walk.

70.

Failure to walk a trail

Comes only when one

Fails to take any more

Steps.

71.

The journey's greatest

Challenge

Is in taking

The final steps.

72.

Great fires rage

When small fires

Are allowed to burn.

73.

The two can be one

When they are of each other

And of themselves.

Such is harmony.

74.

Seek but never claim

To know.

Search but never claim

To possess,

For The One is greater

And can never be claimed.

75.

All things

Are of The One

And cannot be managed.

The self desires many things

But needs only

What is required

To seek The Way.

76.

One should judge

The myriad

As one would judge the family.

One should judge

The family

As one would judge the self.

One should judge the self

As The One judges the myriad.

77.

Non-beauty defines beauty–

Both being part of The One.

To seek beauty through excess

And ornamentation

Is to find non-beauty.

78.

The stream does not

Fear the ocean

For they are of

The same thing.

The living do not fear death

For they are of

The same thing.

79.

Fear

Ceases thought,

Ceases action,

Ceases care,

And brings

That which is feared

Close at hand.

80.

As the energy of life

Comes from The One

So it also returns.

From life comes death.

From death comes life.

Fear not the cycles.

The Society

81.

Order is defined from chaos,

Both being part of

The One.

Chaos binds

What is not destroyed,

While order separates

What is created.

Therefore,

Seek order

At the edge of chaos.

82.

To wear extravagant shoes

While others are barefoot,

To dine on great feasts

While others go hungry,

To build great mansions

While others are homeless

Is discord.

83.

Positive action creates

Positive cycles

And leads to contentment.

Negative action creates

Negative cycles

And leads to despair.

84.

Starlight touches the myriad,

Wind blows to all things:

Each part of The One,

Each no greater than another,

And each of itself.

85.

To follow The Way Is to allow all others

To follow The Way

As each shall choose.

To do not

Causes great discord

And is not The Way.

86.

The One exists

Through all things.

When any part suffers,

All must bear the pain.

When any part hordes,

All must bear the burden.

87.

When one does not have enough,

There is suffering

For one and all.

When one has enough,

There is contentment

For one and all.

When one has too much,

There is burden

For one and all.

88.

Knowing that the self

Is part of the myriad

And that all are of The One,

One realizes that

Advancing the life of one

Advances the life of all

And advancing the life of all

Advances the self.

89.

The survival of one

Is the task of all

But the path beyond

Is the task of the self.

That is the way.

90.

It is the right of each one

To be given the means

By which to survive

In mind, body, and heart

For only beyond survival

Can each seek

The One

As each shall choose.

91.

Those who rule,

Seek to be above the people

And, therefore,

Should not rule.

Those who wish to be

With the people

Should guide the people

But do not wish to rule.

92.

If the aim of competition

Is to exalt the few

And abase the many,

There is discord.

93.

Casting blame creates division.

Division creates discord.

Solutions cannot be sought

Through discord.

Peace abides in unity.

94.

Resolution without compassion

Creates resentment,

Breeds conflict,

Defeats resolution.

95.

All actions have

Consequences.

A ripple in the water

Flows out

Then returns

To its source.

Wisdom is in knowing

How not to empty the stream,

How not to drown.

96.

Division of the myriad

Causes discord.

Discord in mind

Creates prejudice.

Discord in heart

Creates ignorance.

Discord in action

Creates conflict.

97.

Those who know

The Way

As the tree knows

The Way

Use force

Only when forced upon:

To bend but not break,

To lean but not fall.

98.

Peace with the many

Begins with the self.

Seeing one at peace

Causes others to seek peace.

99.

The myriad emanates from

The One

And seeks to return to it:

Thus, cycles are created.

Moving in spirals

Creates change:

The constancy of life.

This is an end

Or a beginning

Or something

Just between.

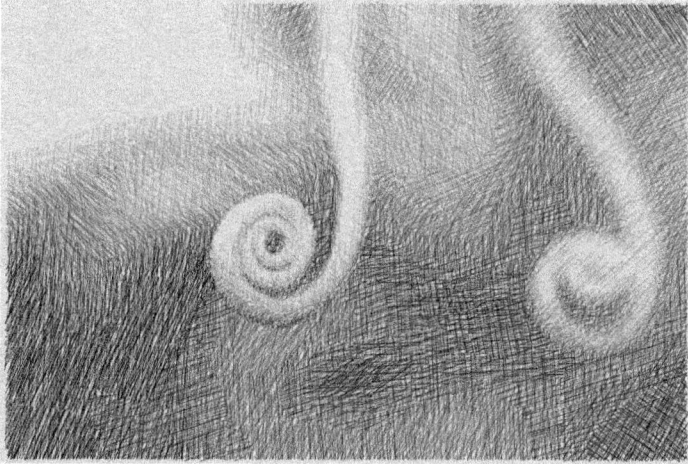

Appendices

Correlation with the Tao Te Ching

Leaf	Tao	Leaf	Tao	Leaf	Tao	Leaf	Tao
1	42	26	47	51	38	76	54
2	14	27	44	52	38	77	41
3	6	28	20	53	13	78	74
4	47	29	53	54	13	79	50
5	11	30	25	55	11	80	50
6	59	31	51	56	42	81	18
7	48	32	41	57	10	82	53
8	14	33	81	58	63	83	26
9	48	34	33	59	70	84	32
10	7	35	47	60	49	85	27
11	8	36	71	61	12	86	75
12	34	37	56	62	21	87	9
13	78	38	16	63	23	88	7
14	21	39	56	64	76	89	51
15	81	40	9	65	62	90	46
16	41	41	36	66	58	91	66
17	55	42	2	67	63	92	3
18	48	43	61	68	45	93	79
19	19	44	35	69	43	94	79
20	15	45	12	70	64	95	30
21	69	46	52	71	64	96	46
22	41	47	2	72	64	97	31
23	63	48	77	73	28	98	54
24	48	49	52	74	67	99	40
25	1	50	44	75	46		

Index of Topics

Other Books

Non-Fiction

- Spirituality
  - A Different Calling: A Manual for Lay Ministers and Other Non-Professional Facilitators of Any Spiritual Tradition
  - Many Leaves, One Tree: A Collection of Aphorisms Inspired by the Tao Te Ching
  - The Purpose Derived Life: What In The Universe Am I Here For?
  - Three Guidelines for Ethical Living
  - Playing Cards and the Game of Living Well
  - The Emergence of God: The Intersection of Science, Nature, and Spirituality
  - The Langer Deck
  - Emergent Spirituality: Principles and Practices at the Intersection of Science, Nature, and Spirituality
  - Open Hearts and Open Doors: Radical Hospitality in the Church
  - Let Us Wander: A Ministry of Music and Arts
- Games
  - 52 New Card Games (For Those Old Cards)
  - 36 New Dice Games
  - 40 Games for Forty Dice
  - Castle Imbroglio: An Escape Adventure Book
- Music
  - A Guide to the Art of Musical Performance
  - A Theory for All Music

- - Book 1: Fundamentals
  - Book 2: Chords and Part-Writing
  - Book 3: The Tools of Analysis
  - Book 4: Parametric Analysis
  - Rounds and Canons for Peace and Justice
  - Music for Unitarian-Universalist Choirs
  - Songs of Worship
  - 50 Songs for Meditation

Fiction

- Science Fiction
  - The Milleran Cluster Series
    - Of Eternal Light
    - The Forever Horizon
    - The Suicide Fire
    - The Song of the Mother
    - The Journey of Awri
- Theater
  - Four Comedies
  - 10 x 10: Ten Ten-Minute Plays Book 1
  - 10 x 10: Ten Ten-Minute Plays Book 2
  - 10 x 10: Ten Ten-Minute Plays Book 3
  - 10 x 10:Ten Ten-Minute Plays Book 4
  - Ageless Wisdom: Multigenerational Plays for Worship
- Poetry
  - Looking At The World: A Collection of Poetry

  - Prayers

About The Author

Kenneth P. Langer

Rev. Dr. Kenneth P. Langer is an ordained Universalist minister and a former college professor with graduate degrees in both music and theology. He is a published writer, composer, and poet and is the author of several works of fiction as well as books on spiritual living. He also enjoys playing and designing games.

Learn more by visiting his website:
http://kennethplanger.com

Final Note

Thank you for reading this book!

If you enjoyed reading it please let me know
and please consider writing a positive online review.

Ken Langer

Contact Information
personal website: http://kennethplanger.com
book site: http://brassbellbooks.com

www.ingramcontent.com/pod-product-compliance
Lightning Source LLC
Chambersburg PA
CBHW032138040426
42449CB00005B/304